Chasing Lilly Curriculum and Discussion Workbook

Nealie Rose

Chasing Lilly Curriculum and Discussion Workbook,
by Nealie Rose
Copyright 2015/JARI LLC/All Rights Reserved
www.nealierose.com/
email: nealierose@nealierose.com

I sincerely hope that this book will help families, therapists, social workers, foster parents, and teachers to be better prepared for the Lilly's of the future. Thank you for staying with me, and allowing me the opportunity to share this story with you. Love my readers,
Nealie Rose

Discussion Questions, Thesis Topics, and Answers are at the end.

CHAPTER 1

1. What was the culture question that Tana asked her class?

2. What was her response?

3. Name three possible scenarios that could place a child in foster care.

CHAPTER 2

1. Did Lilly remove her coat in the hospital pharmacy?

2. Why or why not?

CHAPTER 3

1. What 9 things required that Bruce and Nealie fill out a Critical Incident Report?

2. What does RAD stand for?

3. What causes it?

4. What fear goes with RAD?

CHAPTER 4

1. What had Lilly been doing to survive at age two?

2. This caused her to _____

   _____.

CHAPTER 5

1. Why did Nealie describe Lilly as a "kid of many colors?"

2. What did Nealie take away from Lilly in the car?

3. What saved the day?

4. Explain the visual swimming pool teaching tool.

CHAPTER 6

1. List nine people who were in the picture when Lilly came to live with Bruce and Nealie Rose.

CHAPTER 7

1. What was the purpose of Kathi's play therapy with the cats?

CHAPTER 8

1. Who was buried and dug up again?

CHAPTER 9

1. Why was Lilly removed from Ann and Marty Wells' home?
2. What did Ann give to Nealie?

CHAPTER 10

1. Is RAD a common condition?
2. Do most kids in foster care have it?
3. What did Mr. Garth say that infuriated Nealie?
4. What quote of Albert Schweitzer's is mentioned in this chapter?

CHAPTER 11

1. What did Lilly destroy that belonged to Cookie?

CHAPTER 12

1. What did Lilly always include in her prayers?

CHAPTER 13

1. If people walked by Lilly's window and did not smile at her, what would she do?

CHAPTER 14

1. What happened to the carpet in Lilly's room?
2. What toy did Nealie buy for Lilly in this chapter?
3. Why were the outdoor consequences not working?
4. What garage sale item did Nealie find in the washer?

CHAPTER 15

1. The cats' names were _____ and _____.

2. List the five signs that Lilly was on the edge.

3. How did Nealie get Lilly to stop stealing her drink?

CHAPTER 16

1. Who joined the household, and why?

2. What two things did she have to do first?

3. Who was doing day-respites?

4. Why was Nealie so upset when Tibby said that Lilly couldn't come to the party?

CHAPTER 17

1. Name the two movie characters that Lilly would call Nealie.

2. What happened to Lilly's underwear?

CHAPTER 18

1. What does SBH stand for?

2. What does IEP stand for?

3. What was stolen from the porch?

4. Where did Nealie find the top of the chocolate pecan pie?

CHAPTER 19

1. Where did Baler and Peek live when Lilly was at home?

CHAPTER 20

1. What was Lilly's question to Nealie about the rocking chair?

2. What was Nealie's reply?

3. Why did Lilly need to pause and think about Nealie's response?

CHAPTER 21

1. What is chapter 21 about? _____

   _____.

2. Who was John?

CHAPTER 22

1. Regarding the conversation overheard in the Italian restaurant, how did Lilly come to her conclusion?

CHAPTER 23

1. Why did Lilly hit Danny?
2. What was a problem when the IEP evaluators were observing Lilly?

CHAPTER 24

1. What was Lilly's core belief?
2. What was Tina's one sin?
3. Why was the Substance Abuse box checked on the Critical Incident Reports?

CHAPTER 25

1. What did Miss Coops say to Lilly?
2. Why was that so wrong?

CHAPTER 26

1. What was the lesson that Nealie was trying to teach Lilly about stealing?
2. How was Lilly catching flies?

CHAPTER 27

1. Why did Nealie think that Miss Coops may have been relieved to see Lilly move on?

2. Why did Nealie feel that Mrs. Firm's relief was mixed with feelings of partial failure?

3. What do you think could help the situation if there could be a re-do? Give at least two thoughts.

CHAPTER 28

1. Why was the Life Book important?

CHAPTER 29

1. After reading this chapter, what thoughts do you come away with?

CHAPTER 30

1. What would you do if you were working, counseling, or teaching, and a child pulled your hair and wouldn't let go?

CHAPTER 31

1. What question nagged at Nealie?
2. Nealie thought that Lilly's cutting was a spin-off of what?

CHAPTER 32

1. How did spring-cleaning go?
2. What was Lilly's reply to Bob when he asked her why she wrote on the wall?
3. Why is her reply so interesting?

CHAPTER 33

1. Do you think that Lilly should have gone to Camp Hope?
2. Why or why not?

CHAPTER 34

1. Why do you think Sasha's approach to Lilly's screaming and shouting worked?
2. What did Lilly put in her ear?

CHAPTER 35

1. What main problem was the bus driver having with Lilly?
2. Was Lilly obsessed with Pete's whereabouts?

CHAPTER 36

1. What was one good thing that came from the hospitalization?

CHAPTER 37

1. What cracked in this chapter?

CHAPTER 38

1. What was Lilly's conclusion about herself?
2. How many days was Lilly in the hospital in May and June?

CHAPTER 39

1. What two things did Lilly use to try to harm herself?

CHAPTER 40

1. What was the big doctor problem?
2. Why wasn't Lilly in her class picture?

CHAPTER 41

1. What was the breakthrough in this chapter?

CHAPTER 42

1. Lilly said that something made Abraham rich. What was it?
2. Okay, you are at the pool with Lilly, and you are Nealie. What would you have done?

CHAPTER 43

1. Nealie said that they had no control over what?
2. What was Lilly throwing at people?

CHAPTER 44

1. Was Mayfair as bad as Nealie had imagined?

2. How long was Lilly missing?

3. What was strapped to the police car?

4. Why do you think that as a rule, social workers do not go with foster parents in the same vehicle?

CHAPTER 45

1. Why was Nealie being so difficult?

CHAPTER 46

1. Why was Lilly angry not long after Christmas?

2. What happened to her right hand?

3. What did Pete think that his attacker was doing?

4. Fill in the blank:

    If you cut your clothes to ribbons

    and run _____ in the park

    I would feel _____ for you

    and would hope you'd wait 'till _____ ."

CHAPTER 47

1. What did Nealie do to "help" Lilly, at Dan's urging?

2. How long was Lilly at Mayfair?

CHAPTER 48

1. Please write your thoughts on the adoption of the two brothers in one or two paragraphs.
2. What tool helped keep tabs on Lilly?

CHAPTER 49

1. Was choir a success for Lilly?
2. What did she cut?

CHAPTER 50

1. What was the terrifying report from the dispatcher?
2. Lilly wanted a particular food, and her behavior was triggered when she didn't get what?
3. Who filled the page on Lilly's picture?

CHAPTER 51

1. What did Lilly confess to?
2. Did she know her phone number?
3. What was the cat's name?
4. Why did Lilly seem relieved when the doctor talked about prescription changes?

CHAPTER 52

1. What did Lilly steal?

CHAPTER 53

1. Why were the pajamas significant to Nealie?
2. Who was Sammy?
3. What dawned on Nealie in this chapter, regarding Dan Wheatley?

CHAPTER 54

1. What did Dan want Bruce and Nealie to tell Lilly?

CHAPTER 55

1. Why was Lilly being moved from Mayfair?
2. Bruce and Nealie had to remind themselves of what two things?

CHAPTER 56

1. What news upset and shocked Nealie?
2. Did Lilly progress to a step-down unit?
3. Why was Lilly trying cottage doors to get inside?

CHAPTER 57

1. What did Lilly steal at a drugstore, and what did she do with it?

2. What was Lilly's doll's name?

CHAPTER 58

1. Did Lilly believe that she had hurt the dog?

DISCUSSION QUESTIONS

1. Do you think that it is okay to put a fence around a yard to keep children from wandering?

2. Do you think that children on a bus should wear a harness to secure them if they refuse to stay in their seats and/or harm other children?

3. Do you think that it was okay for Nealie to use a baby gate in Lilly's doorway?

4. Do you think that it is okay to put breathable netting "roof" over a toddler's crib if they won't stay in it at night?

5. Do you think it is okay for parents to confine a violent or destructive child to one area?

6. How big should that area be?

7. For how long should they be confined?

8. Would your thoughts change if that child had grown to be uncontrollable, and was dangerous?

9. When states phase out long-term residential facilities to save money, where should these people be placed, and for how long?

THESIS TOPICS

1. The home and school use of barriers and enclosures for violent people.

2. Non-treatment of Reactive Attachment Disorder in relation to crimes committed.

3. Housing/placement of violent children in society, and aging-out decisions.

4. Foster care versus orphanages or "children's villages."

5. Foster care versus adoption outcomes.

6. The argument for respite for any family with RAD children.

7. Who decides what to do when an adoption does not work out? Next step guidelines and policy. Re-homing alternatives.

ANSWERS

CHAPTER 1
1. What determines a person's culture?
2. You culture is how you were raised. I was a Black girl, raised around Whites. My culture was White. Culture is not defined by your skin color.
3. abuse, abandonment, parental drug addiction, parental prostitution

CHAPTER 2
1. No
2. She was afraid that she would be left behind.

CHAPTER 3
1. hospitalization, injury, theft, runaway, unusual violence, sexual assault or misbehavior, harm to pets, self-harming, destruction of property
2. Reactive Attachment Disorder
3. Severe loss and lack of attachment with a lasting parental figure causes RAD.
4. A huge fear of MORE hurt or loss if they become close to, or attached to another parental figure.

CHAPTER 4
1. She was looking in garbage cans for food.
2. hoard food

CHAPTER 5
1. Lilly had written on her face with markers.
2. Polly the parrot.
3. a beetle sighting.
4. The empty pool is a life of a child. The bucket of dirt is the trauma (or bad) in their life. The foster parent's job was to dilute the dirt with buckets of goodness and love, so that the bad would not matter as much, and the child could go on to have a fulfilling and empowered life.

CHAPTER 6
1. Tina
2. Ann and Marty Wells
3. psychiatrist
4. registered nurse
5. CHC worker
6. therapist
7. play therapist
8. county worker
9. guardian ad litem

CHAPTER 7
1. The therapy reinforced over and over that a good mother will protect her child. (A good mother tiger would protect her cubs or kittens.) Mothers protect their children.

CHAPTER 8
1. Karina

CHAPTER 9
1. Lilly kicked Ann's abdomen, which caused vaginal bleeding.
2. three letters

CHAPTER 10
1. no
2. no
3. "If she's not eating, then I don't want to eat."
4. "Anyone who has accustomed himself to regard the life of any living creature as worthless is in danger of arriving also at the idea of worthless human lives." Albert Schweitzer

CHAPTER 11
1. a plastic horse

CHAPTER 12
1. "Thank you for me."

CHAPTER 13
1. Lilly would give them the middle finger.

CHAPTER 14
1. It was rolled up and taken out after Lilly peed on it.
2. a ball
3. The outdoor consequences were not working because when they were announced, Lilly would take off running!
4. a ring

CHAPTER 15
1. Baler and Peek
2. pacing, increased thumb-sucking, hunched shoulders, head tipped down, and trying to control everything
3. Nealie played a trick on Lilly that involved putting soy sauce and ice in a glass to make it look like cola.

CHAPTER 16
1. Hannah joined the household because she needed a place to stay.
2. Hannah had to be finger-printed and have a background check.
3. Mary and Roger Stevens
4. Nealie was upset because she felt that she had lost the support of her family, which mattered very much because she and Bruce had lost their social circle.

CHAPTER 17
1. Henry Higgins and Cruella Deville
2. Lilly flushed the panties down the toilet.

CHAPTER 18
1. Severe Behavior Handicapped
2. Individual Educational Plan
3. the bouncing horse
4. in an afghan in the den

CHAPTER 19
1. in the basement

CHAPTER 20
1. "Why do you have to rock me?"
2. "Because I want you to know that I love you, and I am so proud of you when you are a good girl."
3. The response was not what she expected. The response had the effect of encouragement rather than disappointment.

CHAPTER 21
1. the glasses
2. Nobody knows!

CHAPTER 22
1. Lilly knew abuse from her birth mother, thus if a mother was abusive, she must be a birth mother.

CHAPTER 23
1. He must have irritated her when he sang to her.
2. Lilly would behave much better when they were doing an evaluation. RAD kids behave better with strangers.

CHAPTER 24
1. Lilly's core belief was that the world was bad and so were most people in it. If they weren't bad, then they still needed to be kept at arm's length in case they turned bad.
2. Tina had pushed Lilly down some stairs.
3. Because there was no box for feces-smearing.

CHAPTER 25
1. Miss Coops told Lilly that the devil was in her heart.
2. This was wrong for more than one reason:
It was mean.
It targeted a vulnerable child.
It was the last thing Lilly needed to hear on her way to healing from abuse.
It proved detrimental to Lilly's healing process and progress.

CHAPTER 26
1. Nealie was trying to teach empathy, or how it felt to be on the other end of a theft, as in when *your* things were taken.

2. Lilly used dog doo as bait and she slammed a bowl down over the flies that landed.

CHAPTER 27
1. Nealie thought that Miss Coops felt terrible that she had messed up so badly, and the constant reminder of having Lilly in her class would be gone.
2. Nealie thought that Mrs. Firm had experienced a new low in her lengthy career, and that she felt partly responsible for Lilly's failure in class.
3. *Leave your own thoughts in response to this question.*

CHAPTER 28
1. The Life Book was important because it helped Lilly piece together her fragmented life, and gave her a sense of self.

CHAPTER 29
1. *Leave your own thoughts in response to this question.*

CHAPTER 30
1. *Leave your own thoughts in response to this question.*

CHAPTER 31
1. Why hadn't Lilly broken the big picture window in her room?
2. Head-banging when she was younger.

CHAPTER 32
1. A complete disaster.
2. "Don't you know I have problems?"
3. She was aware that she had issues, and many of us are not.

CHAPTER 33
1. *Leave your own thoughts in response to this question.*
2. *Leave your own thoughts in response to this question.*

CHAPTER 34
1. *Leave your own thoughts in response to this question.*
2. a beetle or beetles

CHAPTER 35
1. The bus driver couldn't get her to stay in her seat, even with the harness.
2. no

CHAPTER 36
1. CHC found another children's psychiatrist.

CHAPTER 37
1. Nealie's halo

CHAPTER 38
1. Her conclusion about herself was that she was bad, mad, and sad.
2. 19

CHAPTER 39
1. rubbing alcohol and rat poison

CHAPTER 40
1. The problem was that the hospital doctor did not treat out-patients, and the regular doctor didn't treat in-patients. There was no overlapping care, and both doctors had their own course of treatment.
2. She must have been with the Help Team because of a melt-down.

CHAPTER 41
1. Lilly told Nealie, "I love you."

CHAPTER 42
1. His flop of cheeps made him so rich.
2. *Leave your own thoughts in response to this question.*

CHAPTER 43
1. Nealie said that they had no control over other people's lives, or the fact that time was marching on.
2. patio rocks

CHAPTER 44
1. no
2. eight long hours
3. a girl's pink bike

4. Basically, they have to maintain professional standards and barriers in order to do their job.

CHAPTER 45
1. Nealie felt like someone had stolen her child. She had somehow 'lost' her.

CHAPTER 46
1. Lilly's device was stolen from her room.
2. It was broken, supposedly by a mean staff member.
3. Pete thought the kid was wrestling with him.
4. naked, embarrassed, dark

CHAPTER 47
1. Nealie hid under a sheer fabric to play Hide and Seek.
2. 10 months

CHAPTER 48
1. *Leave your own thoughts in response to this question.*
2. walkie talkies

CHAPTER 49
1. yes
2. Lilly cut the cords on all electrical equipment.

CHAPTER 50
1. Lilly had jumped out of the van and was running up the busy highway throwing stones at cars.
2. brownies
3. God

CHAPTER 51
1. Lilly confessed to drinking the neighbor's beer.
2. no
3. Johnny Cash
4. Lilly seemed relieved because she wanted something to help her. She wanted a medicine to help.

CHAPTER 52
1. Lilly stole the neighbor's dog.

CHAPTER 53
1. The pajamas were significant because if they all left with Lilly, then that meant that Lilly was gone from her home. There was no need for pajamas if you didn't live and sleep there.
2. a stuffed seal
3. Nealie realized that all of this was hard on him, as well.

CHAPTER 54
1. Dan wanted Bruce and Nealie to tell Lilly that she would not be going back to their house to live.

CHAPTER 55
1. Lilly was turning thirteen, and Mayfair was for up to age thirteen.
2. Lilly's behavior put her there, and she could earn her way to a step-down unit.

CHAPTER 56
1. Roger Stevens was arrested for sexual abuse of a foster boy.
2. yes
3. Lilly was trying to get in because she had been sprayed by a skunk.

CHAPTER 57
1. Lilly stole some black hair dye, and she dyed her hair with it in a gas station bathroom.
2. Jasmine

CHAPTER 58
1. no, not really

www.ingramcontent.com/pod-product-compliance
Lightning Source LLC
Chambersburg PA
CBHW061313040426
42444CB00010B/2625